The Dred Scott Case

Slavery and Citizenship

The Dred Scott Case
Slavery and Citizenship

D.J. Herda

Landmark Supreme Court Cases

ENSLOW PUBLISHERS, INC.

44 Fadem Road	P.O. Box 38
Box 699	Aldershot
Springfield, N.J. 07081	Hants GU12 6BP
U.S.A.	U.K.

T 25086

Library of Congress Cataloging-in-Publication Data

Herda, D.J., 1948–
    The Dred Scott case : slavery and citizenship / D.J. Herda.
       p. cm. — (Landmark Supreme Court cases)
    Includes bibliographical references and index.
    Summary: Describes the people involved on both sides of the famous
Supreme Court case, regarding whether or not slaves had rights as
citizens of the United States.
    ISBN 0-89490-460-4
    1. Scott, Dred, 1809-1858—Trials, litigation, etc.—Juvenile
literature. 2. Slavery—Law and legislation—United States—
Juvenile literature. 3. Slavery—United States—Legal status of
slaves in free states—Juvenile literature. [1. Scott, Dred,
1809-1858. 2. Slavery—Law and legislation.] I. Title.
II. Series.
KF228.S27H47 1994
342.73'087—dc20
[347.30287]   93-22402
                                         CIP
                                         AC

Printed in the United States of America

10 9 8 7 6 5 4 3

Illustration Credits: Culver Pictures, Inc. pp. 9, 13, 16, 24, 27, 30, 37, 40, 49, 55,
61, 66, 72, 79; United States Supreme Court, p. 91.

Cover Photos: Franz Jantzen, "Collection of the Supreme Court of the United
States" (background); Library of Congress (insert).

Contents

1

Missouri, 1840

Dred Scott cradled his daughter, Eliza, in his arms as his wife, Harriet, loaded the last of their meager possessions into the wagon that would carry them to a steamboat bound for St. Louis, Missouri. His second daughter, Lizzie, climbed aboard, and as Scott lifted the youngest child into the hands of the oldest, Harriet began to cry. But hers were not tears of sadness. They were tears of joy. The Scotts were going home.[1]

"Come along now," Dr. Emerson called. "No time for that. We've a long trip ahead of us."

"Yes-suh," Scott replied. "Yes-suh, we sure do." Scott helped his wife aboard, then climbed over the spoked wooden wheel after her. As the two settled down with their daughters, Emerson gave the order to move out, and the wagon lurched suddenly forward.[2]

It was spring, 1840, in Fort Snelling, Minnesota, part of the sprawling Wisconsin Territory. Scott had accompanied John Emerson, an army physician, from Missouri two years earlier. While in the North, Scott had met and married Harriet. Now they were returning home to St. Louis. Not to their home, but to Emerson's home—for Scott, his wife, and their daughters were slaves.

Slavery was still an important part of the economy of the South in 1840. Although slavery had long been banned north of a line roughly equal to the southern boundary of the state of Missouri, Congress, in passing the Missouri Compromise of 1821, had created a special exemption for that state, allowing it to retain slavery.

The issue nonetheless remained a thorn in the side of northern political leaders, who saw slavery as an immoral and shameful institution. Southern leaders, on the other hand, needed inexpensive slave labor to help run their cotton, tobacco, and rice plantations.[3]

By 1840, the debate over slavery had mostly died down. But Dred Scott was destined to change all that, just as he was destined to change his own future, and that of his country- -forever.

Dred Scott was born in Virginia of Negro slaves around 1800. The exact date was never recorded—not an unusual circumstance surrounding the birth of slaves. He

In this photo from Frank Leslie's *Illustrated Newspaper* of June 27, 1857, Dred Scott's youngest daughter, Eliza, is shown on the left. Lizzie, Dred Scott's oldest daughter, is shown on the right.

was the property of Peter Blow, a Virginia farmer who, in 1818, sold his 860 acres and moved with his wife, Elizabeth, his family, and his slaves to a cotton plantation near Huntsville, Alabama. Two years later, Blow moved again, this time to nearby Florence, Alabama. Finally, in 1830, he moved once again, this time settling for good in the bustling riverfront town of St. Louis, "the gateway to the West," on the mighty Mississippi River.

In St. Louis, the Blow family had to adapt to a completely different lifestyle. Rural Virginia and Alabama had been predominantly cotton-growing country, but St. Louis with its excellent port facilities was geared almost exclusively toward commerce, trade, and manufacturing. Blow rented a large home for twenty-five dollars a month and opened a boarding house, which he named the Jefferson Hotel. There Dred Scott and the other Blow slaves worked not in the fields, planting and hoeing and picking cotton, but in the hotel, cleaning and cooking and running errands. It was quite a change for Scott, who had never known anything besides farming, and he found the work easier and less tedious than the field work he had left behind.

In 1831, tragedy struck the Blow family when Peter Blow's wife, Elizabeth, died of a lingering disease. Early the next year, Blow sold the hotel and moved his family into another house. In the months that followed, his own health failed, and Blow finally died on June 23, 1832, leaving the family fortunes in the hands of his eleven children.[4] Although no records exist of Scott's activities during the next few years, Scott himself once referred to the Blow children as "them boys" with whom he had been "raised." From this, it seems likely that Scott had been not only a slave, but also a good friend of the Blow family, especially the third son, Taylor, who would remain a lifelong supporter of Scott.[5]

In late 1833, Blow's daughter Elizabeth apparently sold Dred Scott to Dr. John Emerson, a St. Louis physician approximately Scott's own age. Emerson had moved to St. Louis in 1831 and had quickly befriended such well known local figures as Missouri's U.S. senators Thomas Hart Benton and Alexander Buckner, as well as Dr. William Carr Lane, the first mayor of St. Louis, William H. Ashley, a Missouri congressman, and several members of the Missouri state legislature. Indeed, Emerson seems to have been better suited to making influential friends than to practicing medicine, a skill in which he seems to have been poorly trained and only marginally effective.[6]

Nonetheless, on October 25, 1833, Emerson, who had applied for a position with the U.S. Army, was accepted into the armed forces and appointed to the position of assistant surgeon. But it was not his skill alone that got him the appointment. Just when it looked as though Emerson would be passed by once again (he had been trying to gain a commission for years), the physician asked some of his most influential friends to come to his aid. Thirteen members of the Missouri state legislature signed a letter recommending him, as did Senator Benton. The following month, Emerson received new orders and moved to Fort Armstrong, Illinois, taking Scott with him. There, the physician reported to his commander, Lieutenant-Colonel William Davenport, to begin what would eventually become a nine-year military career.

But life at Fort Armstrong proved less than comfortable. The fort's old log buildings were rotted and falling apart, and the roofs of the soldiers' barracks leaked with every rain. Undoubtedly, the slaves' quarters were even worse. Yet, despite frequent outbreaks of cholera and other diseases, Scott remained at Emerson's side, "in service" to the physician "as a slave and used by him as such"[7]—this despite the fact that Illinois had prohibited slavery since 1787, when the Congress of the Confederation passed the Northwest Ordinance, which banned slavery in the region. Scott might possibly have sued for his freedom, had it occurred to him to do so, on the grounds that he was living in a free territory. But, for

Thomas H. Benton served as a United States senator from Missouri for thirty years. He joined Missouri's government just as it joined the Union as a state in 1821.

some reason he did not. Instead, he stayed at his master's side.

Meanwhile, Emerson was far from pleased with life on the plains. Within two months of his arrival at Fort Armstrong, he asked his commander for a leave of absence, claiming that he had contracted a "syphiloid disease" during a visit to Philadelphia. When that failed to produce the results he desired, Emerson once again enlisted his friends to begin placing pressure on the War Department to transfer him back to St. Louis. Emerson himself informed the department that his left foot had developed a "slight disease" that might require surgery. In January 1836, he tried again, complaining that he'd had an argument with one of his company commanders and could no longer work for the man.[8]

Despite his dissatisfaction with his position, Emerson did reap some rewards from his assignment. He bought several acres of land near the fort, along with an entire section across the Mississippi River, near present-day Davenport, Iowa. There, Emerson had Scott build a small cabin.

Finally, the U.S. War Department decided to close Fort Armstrong, partly because of the poor condition of the fort, but mainly because of the worsening situation with the Indian tribes along the western frontier. The fort, the government had decided, was simply no longer capable of protecting the residents of the area in light of the increasing Indian hostilities.

On May 4, 1836, after receiving his reassignment orders, Emerson and Scott were on the move, but not toward St. Louis. Instead, Emerson had been ordered to Fort Snelling, some two hundred miles farther north, in the recently created Wisconsin Territory near present-day St. Paul, Minnesota. Set on the west bank of the Mississippi, the fort was located in a portion of the Louisiana Purchase territory where slavery had been banned by the Missouri Compromise of 1820. Once again, Scott might have sued for his freedom, but again he failed to do so. Instead, he remained in the service of Emerson, apparently never thinking to ask for his release from bondage.[9]

Shortly after arriving at Fort Snelling, Dred Scott's life was destined to change. There he met Major Lawrence Taliaferro, who worked at the Indian Agency near the fort. Taliaferro periodically left the territory to visit friends and relatives in Virginia, often returning with slaves whom he hired out or put to work in the agency. One of these slaves was Harriet Robinson, a young girl in her middle teens. Dred and Harriet became good friends, and soon afterward, they married, despite the fact that Scott was more than twice her age.

Following the ceremony—a rare occurrence for

15

In this illustration of Dred and Harriet Scott, soon after they were married, the difference in their ages is evident. Youthful looking Harriet is greatly contrasted by Dred's older more "fatherly" appearance.

slaves—Taliaferro either gave or sold Harriet to Dr. Emerson. For the next several months, the two slaves worked for Emerson or whomever Emerson hired them out to. Following their first winter in the North, Emerson once again was hard at work petitioning the Surgeon General for reassignment, writing that the cold weather had "crippled him with rheumatism. . . ." He requested either a transfer to St. Louis or six months' leave beginning the following autumn, barely in time to avoid another harsh winter.[10] This time, his request fell on receptive ears, and on October 20, 1837, Emerson was ordered to Jefferson Barracks in St. Louis.

Emerson was elated with his new orders and quickly arranged for a canoe to take him part of the way south, where he could catch a steamboat to St. Louis. He was forced to leave behind most of his belongings and both of his slaves, all of which he planned to send for later.

But when Emerson arrived in St. Louis, he received bad news. His assignment had been changed, and he was now being ordered to Fort Jesup in western Louisiana.

Emerson arrived at Fort Jesup on November 22, 1837. Within two days, he had decided he hated swampy Louisiana even more than the frigid Northlands and wrote a request for transfer back to Fort Snelling, which, by comparison, looked suddenly good to him. Over the next few weeks, the doctor wrote several more letters explaining the undue hardships he was forced to endure in Louisiana. The damp climate had revived an old liver disorder, he claimed. Rheumatism had reared its ugly head and was causing him difficulty in breathing.

Yet, despite his weakened physical condition, Emerson somehow managed to find the strength to pursue a whirlwind courtship, and he married the twenty-three-year-old Eliza Irene Sanford, some fifteen years his junior, on February 6, 1838. Soon after the ceremony, Emerson sent for Dred and Harriet Scott.

Following his honeymoon, Emerson again tried to get transferred from Fort Jesup. Once again, the Surgeon General gave in to Emerson's badgering, possibly hoping to end once and for all the stream of letters pouring across his desk.[11] That September, Emerson was transferred back to Fort Snelling. After a brief stopover in St. Louis, the Emersons and their slaves boarded the steamliner *Gypsy* for the trip north. Another passenger on board, a Methodist missionary, later recalled in his memoirs, "Among the passengers were Dr. Emerson and his wife, having with them their servants, Dred Scott and his family, who belonged to this lady. On the upward trip one of Dred's children, a girl, was born."[12] Eliza Scott had been born in free territory north of the Missouri state line.

Once back at Fort Snelling, Emerson remained there

for two years until the outbreak of fighting with the Seminole Indians prompted his transfer to Florida in the spring of 1840. On the way to Cedar Key, Florida, Emerson dropped off his wife and slaves in St. Louis, where they would be safe. Emerson served as a medical officer in the Seminole Wars for more than two years. During this time he sent repeated letters to the Surgeon General, complaining of recurring fever and other illnesses and requesting a transfer north. *Anywhere* north. Finally, with the end of the war, the Surgeon General, taking advantage of an order to reduce the size of the army's medical staff, gave Emerson an honorable discharge. Emerson suddenly found himself back in civilian life.

Following the discharge, Emerson's life took a turn for the worse. Unable to succeed in private practice in St. Louis, he decided to move with his wife to Davenport in Iowa Territory. There he opened a private practice, bought two city lots, and began building a brick house. By now, his wife was expecting a child. But Emerson's health soon began to fail, and he died at the age of forty, just one month after the birth of his daughter, Henrietta.

Emerson willed all of his property to his wife. Mrs. Emerson, who had little need for slaves herself, hired out Dred and Harriet Scott to her brother-in-law, Captain Henry Bainbridge, who kept the Scotts in his service until March 1846. He apparently took Dred Scott with him to Texas. Upon their return, Scott tried to purchase freedom for himself and his family, but Mrs. Emerson refused, hiring them out instead to Samuel Russell of St. Louis.

The following month, on April 6, 1846, Dred and Harriet Scott filed petitions in the Missouri Circuit Court, outlining their former residence on free soil and requesting permission to file suit against Irene Emerson to establish their right to freedom. The judge granted them the right to sue, and on that very same day, the Scotts filed actions for assault and false imprisonment. Dred's complaint stated that on April 4, 1846, Mrs. Emerson had "beat, bruised and ill-treated" him and had imprisoned him for twelve hours. The complaint also stated that Dred was entitled to be considered a "free person" who had been held in slavery by the defendant, Mrs. Emerson. It claimed damages of ten dollars.[13]

After living for nearly half a century as a slave, Dred Scott had finally taken the first steps toward freedom. They would function as a turning point in his life. But the suit would eventually turn out to be much larger than that of one man and his wife seeking their freedom. It would soon become the rallying point of a nation . . . and the beginning of one of the most violent eras in American history.

2
Slavery in America

America had undergone many changes since the introduction of slavery to the colonies in 1619. One thing, though, had not changed in the nearly two centuries prior to Dred Scott's birth—the South's need for slaves.

To those living in the North, southern slavery seemed a relatively simple answer to an economic problem. It was a way of life. While most Northerners did not approve of slavery on moral principle, they nonetheless grudgingly acknowledged a need for its existence.[1]

To white southern slave owners, however, slavery was much more than an economic necessity. It was both an answer to the question of where to obtain cheap labor to work the cotton, rice, and tobacco fields and a complex socioeconomic structure upon which the southern states based their very existence. The entire way of life of Southerners depended upon the sweat and toil of enslaved black workers. One South Carolina planter summed up the feelings of his countrymen this way: "Slavery with us is no abstraction but a great and vital fact. Without it our every comfort would be taken from us. Our wives, our children made unhappy—education, the light of knowledge—all, all lost and our people ruined forever."[2]

As time passed and the institution of slavery became a common part of southern life, America began to grow from a relatively small community of people concentrated along the eastern seaboard to a rapidly expanding nation destined to settle the land from sea to sea. Following the Louisiana Purchase, French Americans in New Orleans began moving up the Mississippi River to St. Louis and from there into the lowlands of present-day Missouri. They were soon joined by pioneers and farmers from Ohio and Pennsylvania, and the region's population grew rapidly. By 1819, Missouri had attracted so many people that it was able to apply for admission into the Union as a state.

But the state constitution that Missouri submitted for approval by Congress permitted slavery. This set off a heated debate between southern proslavery and northern antislavery forces. The northern states had long since banned the buying and selling of slaves, and most had gone so far as to prohibit slavery with amendments to their state constitutions.

Missouri's request to enter the Union as a slave state posed a serious problem to Congress. Dozens of new states were yet to be formed from the land granted to America by the Louisiana Purchase, as well as that in the sprawling Northwest Territory. Would these future states seeking to enter the Union be slave states or free? In 1819, the number of each of these stood at eleven, providing political balance in Congress. No one group of politicians, proslavery or antislavery, had a majority vote in the Senate.

But when Missouri applied to enter the Union as a slave state, representatives of the northern free states objected. Admitting Missouri to the Union as a slave state would give the proslavery South a senatorial majority. That would provide Southerners with enough votes to pass laws favorable to the South, and unfavorable to the North. Somehow, the ticklish question of slavery and the admission of new states to the Union had to be addressed.

In 1820, Speaker of the House Henry Clay came up with a solution to the problem by offering Congress a compromise. Clay proposed that a line be drawn westward from Missouri's southern border through the

This illustration depicting a slave state on the left-hand side of the picture and a free state on the right-hand side brings to life the raging conflict that future states seeking to enter the Union were forced to faced.

recently acquired Louisiana Territory. All territories north of that line were free to form states in which slavery was prohibited, while all territories to the south would allow slavery. As part of the proposal, Missouri—although situated in the "free zone"—would be exempted and enter the Union as a slave state. The northeastern territory of Maine would enter as a free state, thus keeping the number of slave and free states even. Clay's proposal, known as the Missouri Compromise, was voted upon and accepted by Congress, and Missouri was admitted to the Union as a slave state in 1821.

By 1840, the production of cotton in the southern United States had soared to more than 834 million pounds a year. Cotton had become the single most important crop in the world, king of the entire southern economy.

With the rapid growth of cotton in the southern United States came the spread of the old plantation system that had originally evolved in the Southeast. By 1845, the cotton industry ranged from the Carolinas in the East to eastern Texas in the West and from Tennessee in the North to Florida in the South. As cotton production expanded into the newly admitted slave states of Missouri and Arkansas, these two areas experienced the most rapid growth in the nation.

Although slavery was still legal in the South, antislavery feelings continued to grow nationwide. Those people who were against slavery, called abolitionists, decided to do something to help runaway slaves gain their freedom. They set up a loosely organized system to help runaways escape to Canada. The system was called the Underground Railroad because it provided a secret means of transporting slaves to the North.

When abolitionists working for the "railroad" heard about a runaway slave, they would place the slave under their protection and hide him or her until it was safe to move the slave along to another hiding place, or "station," farther north. From the most heavily populated slave states of Alabama, Mississippi, Louisiana, and Arkansas, runaway slaves traveled this "railroad" through Tennessee, Kentucky, Ohio, and Michigan to safety in Canada. At each hiding place, they were given food and shelter until they were ready to move on. The entire trip might take anywhere from several weeks to two or three months. In this way, the abolitionists helped thousands of slaves to escape to freedom. Their success angered slave owners, who viewed the abolitionists as common thieves out to ruin their way of life.[3]

No doubt Dred Scott had heard about the Underground Railroad, as well as other abolitionist efforts to free the slaves. Even in the closed society of the

The women pictured here were abolitionists, fighting against slavery, prior to the Civil War.

Deep South, news traveled quickly from one plantation to the next. By the mid-1840s, Scott, too, may have been ready for freedom. Now that his two previous masters, Peter Blow and John Emerson, were dead, his own future was in doubt. Would he remain the property of Mrs. Emerson or be sold to someone else? And, if he remained with the Emerson family, would he be shuttled from one job to the next, forced to go wherever he was needed, to work at whatever job had to be done?

Even more important, Scott must have wondered about the fate of his wife and children. It was not unusual in nineteenth-century America for slave families to be broken up and sold to the highest bidders, with husbands and wives, sons and daughters each going their separate ways, never to meet again. Such were the inhumane horrors of slavery.

All of this may have been on Scott's mind when, on April 6, 1846, he filed a suit for his freedom in the Missouri Circuit Court. Dred Scott's long and difficult quest for freedom had begun.

3
Building a Case

Unlike the states farther to the south, Missouri enacted slave laws that were based upon those of Virginia and Kentucky. These laws provided an opportunity for slaves to file suits for freedom. The Scotts were lucky. Had they lived anywhere else in the South, their suits most likely would not have been allowed.

Exactly how the suits of Dred and Harriet Scott began and who started them remains a mystery. Some historians believe that Taylor Blow, Scott's long-time friend and childhood companion, may have played a key role. Others feel the suits may have been started by an attorney who felt he could make a large amount of money from the case. As one historian explained, "[The lawyer's] object was to pave the way for a suit against the Emerson estate for the twelve years' wages to which Scott would be entitled should the courts declare that he had been illegally held as a slave since 1834."[1]

There is also the possibility that it was Scott himself who first decided to sue for his freedom. For a slave, he was well-traveled and quite worldly. Although he could neither read nor write and could only make his "mark" on legal documents and such, many people who knew him praised him openly. A one-time governor of Missouri recalled that "Scott was a very much respected Negro." A St. Louis newspaper reporter, in an article interview with Scott after he had gained considerable notoriety from his suits, described him as "illiterate but not ignorant," with a "strong common sense" that had been honed by years of travel with his masters.[2]

Most likely, Scott decided to bring his case to court after years of discussions with other slaves who had done the same, as well as after several talks with his old friends, the Blows, who were sympathetic to his troubles.

Both the Blows and their in-laws remained Scott's main supporters throughout the slave's life. One of the reasons for this closeness may have been the resentment the Blow children felt when Scott was sold to Emerson. In particular, Taylor Blow, who quite unexpectedly found himself orphaned at the age of twelve, must have felt betrayed. Scott's departure from the Blow family meant the loss of a good friend at a bad time in Taylor's

Dred Scott, shown in this portrait from the Missouri Historical Society, was well-liked and considered worldly, despite the fact that he could neither read nor write.

life. Certainly Taylor remained Scott's most loyal supporter throughout the slave's long fight for freedom, and beyond. In fact, upon Scott's death in 1867, Taylor Blow had his body moved from an abandoned cemetery plot to a more suitable resting place. [3]

Although no historical records prove the fact, it is even possible that the Blows paid for the majority of Scott's legal fees, although Scott himself once stated in an interview that he personally had paid some $500 in cash and about the same amount in labor. Still, the number of lawyers who eventually worked on the case would undoubtedly have earned far more in fees than $1,000.

Regardless of who was responsible for what, the Scotts and their attorneys had a strong case under Missouri law. Time and again, the highest court in the state had found that a master who removed a slave to a free state or territory where slavery was banned had thereby set him free.

Unfortunately for the Scotts, Mrs. Emerson and her attorneys were determined to block Scott's attempt to obtain his freedom. Even more unfortunately, the political atmosphere in Missouri was beginning to shift from one that provided a sympathetic climate for the freeing of slaves to one that was much more closed. The Scotts had no way of knowing it at the time, but this shift in climate would ultimately work its way into the state's courts, and the Scotts would become casualties of the growing division between the slave and free states in America.

The Scotts' cases, virtually identical (and so treated as one in this book), finally came to court on June 30, 1847, with Judge Alexander Hamilton the presiding, or head, judge. Although court records are somewhat unclear, it seems that Scott's attorney, Samuel Mansfield Bay, the former attorney general of Missouri, spoke for the slave. Mrs. Emerson was represented by George W. Goode, a Virginia lawyer with strong proslavery feelings.

On the surface, Scott's attorneys seemed to face a fairly simple task. They needed to prove first that Scott had once lived on free soil and second that he was now held as a slave by Mrs. Emerson, both fairly obvious facts.

In his opening arguments, Bay called witnesses who had known Dred Scott at Forts Armstrong and Snelling. That established the point of Scott's residence on free soil. For the second point, Bay relied mostly on the testimony, or statements taken under oath, of Samuel Russell, who told the court that he had hired the Scotts from Mrs. Emerson, paying Mrs. Emerson's father, Alexander Sanford, money for their use.

Upon cross-examination by Goode, however, Russell admitted that it was actually his wife who had made all the arrangements, and that he, Russell, knew no more about them than what his wife had told him. That meant that Scott's case was hard to prove, and the jury was told to ignore Russell's testimony. Suddenly, the obvious, that Dred and Harriet Scott were Mrs. Emerson's slaves, turned out to be unprovable. As a result, the jury returned a verdict for the defendant, Mrs. Emerson.

It was a strange twist of fate that, in effect, allowed Mrs. Emerson to keep her slaves because no one had proved that they *were* her slaves.

Scott's attorneys immediately filed for a new trial, arguing that Russell's testimony had been a surprise to them. Beyond a doubt, Bay insisted, the Scotts could indeed prove that they were slaves.

On December 2, 1847, Judge Hamilton ordered the case to be retried. In response, Mrs. Emerson's lawyer confused the situation further by filing a bill of exceptions to the order for a new trial. The bill was filed because an error had been made in the first trial. If the bill were accepted by the state appellate court, the case would have to be transferred to the Missouri Supreme Court.

In 1848, the Scotts obtained a new team of lawyers from the firm of Alexander P. Field and David N. Hall. Field, in particular, was widely known as a tough prosecutor and had a reputation for winning in the courtroom.[4] Mrs. Emerson, on the other hand, kept Goode as her lawyer. In April 1848, the state appellate court heard the appeal. Two months later, it handed down its decision, declaring that, since an order for a retrial had been made by Circuit Court Judge Hamilton, the Scotts were free to obtain that retrial at the circuit court level. "Granting a new trial cannot be assigned for error,"[5] the decision read in part. The Scotts were delighted to have won something of a victory in the order for a retrial, but meanwhile they had lost valuable time in being sent back to the beginning of their search for freedom.

By now it had become clear that Mrs. Emerson was as determined to keep the Scotts in slavery as the Scotts were to obtain their freedom. Part of the reason may have been that the Blows had by now become bitter enemies of both the Emersons and the Sanfords, and each family was determined to take whatever steps necessary to win, getting caught up in the process in the spirit of battle that a court trial sometimes sparks.

As the retrial drew near, Mrs. Emerson's family hired new attorneys, Hugh A. Garland and Lyman D. Norris, to represent them. The case finally reached the circuit court on January 12, 1850, with Judge Hamilton once again presiding. This time, the Scotts clearly established that they had been hired out to several people by Mrs.

Emerson, thus proving that they were slaves. The jury found in their favor, and the Scotts were, for the moment, declared free.

But Mrs. Emerson had not yet finished fighting. She was unable to get another retrial, so she appealed to the Missouri Supreme Court. At this time, the attorneys for both sides signed an agreement recognizing that, since the cases of Dred and Harriet Scott were virtually identical, they would be combined into a single case. The facts of the case were filed in March 1850, but the court did not hear the case until 1852.

Part of the problem the Scotts faced with the delay was that Missouri was beginning to feel increasing political pressure over the question of slavery. The state found itself in an awkward position, bordered on three sides by free territory. Those opposed to slavery were hard at work just outside Missouri's borders, as well as in critical political offices within the state. These forces placed pressure on Missouri's proslavery legislature, or lawmaking body, to guard against antislavery laws and uprisings.

Set against this unstable political background, the state supreme court judges who heard the case decided to reverse the previous court's decision and reject Scott's claim to freedom. Judge William B. Napton was given the task of writing the court's opinion, which he put off

Antislavery meetings were frequent occurrences in the North. This meeting on the Common in Boston was typical of the organized efforts against slavery.

for several months. In the meantime, new state lawmakers met, and a statewide election removed both Napton and fellow judge James H. Birch from the state supreme court. This meant that their replacements would have to consider the Scott case all over again. It also meant still more time lost—precious time during which those judges who had been leaning toward allowing slaves their freedom were slowly being replaced by more traditional proslavery judges.

So in autumn of 1851, Judge William Scott and Judge Hamilton R. Gamble joined Judge John F. Ryland in reconsidering the Scott case. The results were predictable. On March 22, 1852, Judge Scott handed down his decision. The court found once again in favor of Mrs. Emerson, and it, too, ordered the judgment of the lower court to be reversed. In his opinion, Judge Scott wrote, "Every State has the right of determining how far, in a spirit of comity [or recognition of other state's laws], it will respect the laws of other States. Those laws have no intrinsic [or basic] right to be enforced beyond the limits of the State for which they were enacted. The respect allowed them will depend altogether on their conformity to the policy of our [Missouri] institutions. No State is bound to carry into effect enactments conceived in a spirit hostile to that which pervades her own laws."[6]

Judge Scott went on to declare that conflict of state laws was a matter of judgment, something for the court to consider on a case-by-case basis. Then Judge Scott's opinion moved from legal clarification to a political address, taking on the tone of a school lecture about the value of slavery as a civilizing institution that had raised the American Negro far above the "miserable" African he had previously been. "We are almost persuaded," he continued, "that the introduction of slavery amongst us was, in the providence of God, who makes the evil passions of men subservient to His own glory, a means of placing that unhappy [black] race within the pale of civilized nations."[7]

Judge Scott's decision was as much political as it was legal. It sounded as though Judge Scott were an angry Southern slave owner, not simply an unbiased judge. Nonetheless, the decision stood.

It was a horrible defeat for Dred and Harriet Scott, an amazing victory for Mrs. Emerson. But it was not the end of the Scotts' struggle for freedom. They still had the option of appealing the decision to a higher court.

But the Scotts, for reasons still unknown by historians, failed to file a prompt appeal with the Supreme Court, which would have been the appropriate next step. Instead, they waited until Mrs. Emerson (who by now was remarried to Calvin Chaffee, a staunch

This portrait of an African slave pleading with "Lady Justice" for his freedom, exemplifies the power that Judge Scott and the legal system held over slaves at that time.

opponent of slavery) gave the Scotts to her brother, John Sanford. Then, on November 2, 1853, the Scotts filed their case against Sanford in the Circuit Court of the United States for the District of Missouri. The suit accused Sanford, who was a citizen of New York, of illegally assaulting, holding, and imprisoning Dred Scott, Harriet, and their two daughters, all citizens of Missouri. On that same day, Taylor Blow insured himself to cover "all the costs and fees which may accrue by reason of the prosecution of the said suit,"[8] and the case was set for the April term in 1854.

On April 7, Sanford and his attorney Hugh A. Garland challenged the court's right to hear the case based upon the fact that Dred Scott, as a black man descended from slaves of "pure African blood," had therefore never been a true citizen of Missouri. Judge Robert W. Wells, a former Missouri attorney general, denied the challenge, stating that for the purpose of this case, citizenship implied nothing more than residence in a state.

A free Negro, Wells went on to rule, was enough of a citizen to be able to sue in court. Whether or not Scott was free, Wells pointed out, depended upon the laws that applied to Scott's living in free territory. And that could only be determined after a court hearing.

After lengthy legal planning, the case finally came to

trial on May 15, 1854. Neither Scott's nor Sanford's lawyers called any witnesses or introduced any evidence that had not already been presented to the court. The jury then returned a verdict in Sanford's favor. Somewhat oddly, the trial had gone all too quickly, too routinely. It was as if everyone involved, from the attorneys and the jurors to Judge Wells himself, saw it as the beginning of a challenge in the U.S. Supreme Court.

As expected, once Judge Wells declined a motion for a new trial, Scott's attorney, Alexander Field, filed a bill of exceptions, the first step necessary to take the case to the highest court in the land.

4

To the Highest Court

The circuit court trial had come and gone with little public notice. A brief mention in the *St. Louis Morning Herald* concluded: "Dred is, of course, poor and without any powerful friends. But no doubt he will find at the bar of the Supreme Court some able and generous advocate, who will do all he can to establish his right to go free."[1]

Now the Scotts' work really began. They had to find an attorney who could argue the case before the Supreme Court, preferably an experienced lawyer who was willing to donate his fee for legal services. If that failed, they would need to raise the money themselves—not an easy task. Toward that goal, Scott himself dictated the introduction to a twelve-page pamphlet containing a record of the recent trial:

> I have no money to pay anybody at Washington to speak for me. My fellow-men, can any of you help me in my day of trial? Will nobody speak for me at Washington, even without hope of other reward than the blessings of a poor black man and his family? I do not know. I can only pray that some good heart will be moved by pity to do that for me which I cannot do for myself; and that if the right is on my side it may be so declared by the high court to which I have appealed.[2]

It was an eloquent plea, but it fell on deaf ears. Several months passed, and still Scott had neither an attorney nor the money necessary to pursue the case. Finally, on Christmas Eve, 1854, in a last-ditch effort, Field wrote to Montgomery Blair suggesting that he or some other Washington attorney might serve "the cause of humanity" by taking Scott's case. Blair discussed the matter with his family and friends and then agreed to donate his services as Scott's attorney. He also enlisted the help of *National Era* editor and well-known abolitionist Gamaliel Bailey, who agreed to raise the money necessary for court costs and other related expenses.

In the Kentucky-born Blair, the Scott forces found an extremely able representative. He had been editor of the *Washington Globe* and served with distinction as a member of President Andrew Jackson's cabinet. He had been part of a movement opposing the Kansas-Nebraska Act, passed earlier in 1854, which canceled the antislavery clause of the old Missouri Compromise, opening up a vast new territory to slavery. This delighted most Southerners. Blair's wife was the daughter of a former associate justice of the Supreme Court, and Blair himself had argued many cases before the Court.

But Blair would not have an easy time representing Scott. The two attorneys representing Sanford also had excellent legal qualifications. Both Henry S. Geyer, a respected member of the Missouri State Bar, and Reverdy Johnson, a former senator and attorney general under President Zachary Taylor, were among the most respected constitutional lawyers in the country.

So the battle lines were drawn, and the record, or written notes, of *Dred Scott* v. *Sandford* (the official court spelling) was delivered to the Supreme Court on December 30, 1854.

While Dred Scott was waiting for the Supreme Court's decision, the effects of the just-passed Kansas-Nebraska Act were beginning to take hold. The Act had divided the unsettled land acquired in the Louisiana Purchase into two vast territories, Kansas and Nebraska.

But both Kansas and Nebraska were north of the line created by the Missouri Compromise, which meant that both territories would have been declared free under the Missouri Compromise. Southern representatives naturally objected. The last thing they wanted was a shift of political power to the free states of the North. So, Senator Stephen A. Douglas of Illinois developed a plan to solve the problem.

Early in 1854, Douglas presented a bill to Congress to help create new states from the Louisiana Territory. To win enough votes to get the bill passed into law, he needed to include conditions that appealed to both northern and southern senators. For the proslavery South, Douglas suggested that Congress do away with the Missouri Compromise, with its geographical restrictions on slavery. For the antislavery North, he proposed to leave up to the settlers the question of whether new states formed from the Kansas and Nebraska territories would be free or slave.

The Kansas-Nebraska Act reopened many old wounds about slavery. Most Northerners were against it. They felt that the Missouri Compromise had adequately addressed the question of slavery in new states, and they wanted to keep the old law.

Southerners, on the other hand, liked the new compromise. They realized that Nebraska was too far north ever to become a slave state. But Kansas, with its largely agricultural economy, was a perfect candidate for slavery.

Finally, after several long months of heated debate,

the Kansas-Nebraska Act passed Congress, and the Missouri Compromise was cancelled. Before long, Northerners who were opposed to slavery began encouraging antislavery settlers to move into the territory in an attempt to outvote the settlers who favored slavery. Those opposed to slavery collected funds, paid European immigrants to move to Kansas, and gave the new settlers farm equipment in exchange for their antislavery votes.

Meanwhile, proslavery forces from the South were fighting back. On the day of a scheduled election for Kansas' new lawmakers, some five thousand Southerners swarmed into the territory from nearby Missouri, took control of the voting booths, and cast four times more ballots than there were registered voters in the territory.

Following the election, the solidly proslavery lawmakers met at Shawnee Mission and passed laws favoring slaveholders. These laws limited government office-holders to those who supported slavery. They also provided for the imprisonment of anyone claiming that slavery was either illegal or immoral.

In return, Kansas' antislavery forces held an election of their own to choose delegates to the territory's constitutional convention, which would eventually seek the admission of Kansas to the Union as a free state. As a result, by the end of 1855, Kansas had two separate political communities, each with its own governor, lawmakers, and representatives to Congress. Mixed among the two was a "sprinkling of cutthroats attracted by the promise of trouble, while Southerners could count on support from Missouri 'border ruffians' who were always spoiling to 'clean out the abolition crowd.' "[3]

As the two groups poured into Kansas, the proslavery forces were greeted by threats and even violence. So much blood was shed during the next few months that the territory was soon given the nickname, "Bleeding Kansas."[4]

It was within this explosive political climate that the Supreme Court prepared to hear *Dred Scott* v. *Sanford.* On February 7, 1856, Blair filed his ten-page brief, or summary of the case, for Dred Scott. Dealing first with the facts of the case, Blair argued that, when Scott had gone to Illinois, the Illinois state constitution specifically forbade slavery in that state. Therefore, Blair argued, as soon as Scott set foot in Illinois, he was free from slavery.

But, he asked, was that freedom valid once Scott returned to Missouri? It was, he replied, because of a principle that was valid not only in Missouri, but also in Virginia, Mississippi, and Kentucky, all slave states. It was the principle of permanent emancipation. It meant that, once a slave had been freed, he was free forever. Blair also referred to a previous Supreme Court decision based upon common law principles that said, "liberty,

Scenes like this one, where a proslavery man is seen threatening an abolitionist at gun point, were unfortunately all too common.

once admitted, cannot be recalled," and "once free, always free."[5]

Then Blair turned to a procedural issue, one he thought his opponents would raise in court. Was "a Negro of African descent" a citizen of the United States? Blair admitted that blacks may not have had all rights of U.S. citizenship, but he insisted that they had at least some. His argument was meant to show that Scott had enough of a right as a citizen to sue in court and that Sanford could not claim that the Court lacked authority in the case simply because Scott was a slave.

This is where Blair's brief took a curious turn. Only four pages of the ten-page document were devoted to the main task of proving that Scott had a right to be free because he had lived in Illinois, a free state. The rest of the brief concentrated on winning a point that the lower court had already agreed was valid—that is, that free Negroes were citizens and, thus, qualified to bring suit in a federal court. In short, Blair spent more time and energy defending a point that had already been won than arguing the point that still needed to be won before Scott could be declared free: the principle of permanent emancipation.

Arguments before the Court, with Chief Justice Roger Brooke Taney presiding, began on February 11, 1856, and continued for four days. Blair spoke on the first day, followed by his opponents, Geyer and Johnson, on days two and three, with Blair then receiving a response period for Scott on the fourth day. Since no witnesses were called before the Court, it was not necessary for Dred Scott to attend the sessions, and he stayed in Missouri.

Unfortunately, no detailed record exists of exactly what each of the attorneys said. The Court in those days did not bother to record oral arguments but instead left the matter up to the lawyers as to whether or not they wished to keep such records. Some newspaper reporters who had heard the arguments reported the highlights, writing that Blair spoke "very ably" on behalf of Dred Scott. His argument, they said, was "a calm, learned and conclusive speech."[6] Most likely, the attorney stressed the same two points he had covered in his brief: that a free Negro has the right to sue as a citizen in federal court; and that a slave once given his freedom in a free state remained free even when he returned to a slave state.

Meanwhile, defense attorney Geyer filed his brief on February 8. Although no copy of the brief is known to exist, he probably made the same points the defense had made in previous cases. Three days later, on February 11, the case came up for argument in the Court.

Interestingly enough, few newspapers at the time gave much consideration to the case of Dred Scott, although they carried news of other slave cases, such as the *Sherman Booth* case in Wisconsin, the *Jonathan Lemmon* case in New York, and the *Passmore Williamson* case in Philadelphia. Not even the Washington correspondent for the *St. Louis Daily Missouri Republican* found the *Scott* case important enough to comment on; he wrote not a single word about the case. In fact, the only newspaper to make any mention of substance regarding the case was a Washington paper, which reported, "The public of Washington do not seem to be aware that one of the most important cases ever brought up for adjudication [judgement] by the Supreme Court is now being tried before that august tribunal."[7]

Although no record exists regarding the oral arguments of Sanford's attorneys, Geyer and Johnson, enough was reported in the Washington papers to indicate that they were remarkable in their content.[8] Instead of pursuing the old line of reasoning that Scott was not free because he had lived on a military base or that he had voluntarily returned to the slave state of Missouri or any of the other arguments that had been used in the past, Geyer for the first time tied the *Dred Scott* case to the constitutionality of the Missouri Compromise. He and Johnson argued that Congress did not have the authority to decide the issue of slavery in the territories. Therefore, the Missouri Compromise was unconstitutional and should be reversed, along with its restrictions against slavery. In effect, Geyer argued, Scott had never been a free man because the Missouri Compromise had been invalid. Until that moment, no one had ever before questioned the constitutionality of the Missouri Compromise.[9]

Now, suddenly, the issue before the Court was no longer whether or not Dred Scott would win his freedom; it was whether or not he had ever been free in the first place. And, indeed, if the Missouri Compromise was invalidated by the Court, there would be no basis for Scott's claim that living in Illinois had made him free. Therefore, when Scott returned to Missouri, he still had the same status he had always had—that of a slave.

With these arguments completed, the Court was dismissed to consider the case. On the one hand, the arguments behind Scott's case had been clearly and adequately presented. On the other, Sanford's arguments were equally strong, although the attorneys for Sanford took an entirely new approach to their presentation. Instead of concentrating on the arguments that concerned Scott, the attorneys for Sanford broke new ground.

Scott's Arguments

1. Scott had been a slave in the slave state of Missouri.

2. Scott had traveled to the free state of Illinois, upon which action he became a free man.

3. The principle of permanent emancipation entitled Scott to remain a free man after returning to Missouri; once free, always free, the principle said.

4. Scott indeed had the right to sue for his freedom in federal court because he was a citizen by virtue of his residence in one of the United States of America.[10]

Sanford's Arguments

1. The restrictions on slavery and the Missouri Compromise were invalid because Congress did not have the authority to decide the issue of slavery in the territories.

2. Scott's traveling to Illinois Territory did not, therefore, make him a free man.

3. Scott's return to Missouri, a slave state, meant that since he had never been a free man, he kept his status as a slave.[11]

Dred Scott, shown here, was now the center of his case. No longer were the courts questioning whether or not an uneducated slave could win back his freedom, if he had once lived and worked in a free state. The issue was now whether or not a slave could ever be considered a free citizen at all.

Speculation about the Court's ruling began even before the justices met to consult on the case. If the participants had seemed confused about the differing approaches used by the attorneys, the newspaper reports of the trial were even more confusing. One paper suggested that the Court would be deciding two issues: Congress' authority to control slavery in the territories; and the right of slaveholders to take their slaves into free states without surrendering ownership.[12] Another paper suggested the Court would examine Scott's quest for freedom in light of his voluntary return to Missouri and slavery.[13] Still another insisted that the Court would overlook the question of the constitutionality of the Missouri Compromise and concentrate instead on the right of blacks to be citizens of the United States. [14]

The confusion surrounding what had taken place in the courtroom and how the Court would vote was reflected in a larger sense by the confusion in Congress over the entire slavery issue. In passing both the Missouri Compromise and the Kansas-Nebraska Act, Congress had decided that disputes over slavery and personal freedom should be appealed directly to the Supreme Court, thus avoiding the legalities of slavery. Surprisingly, not until Geyer's attack in his oral arguments had the matter come before the Court. Although *Dred Scott* had begun as a relatively simple question of one man's right to freedom, it had suddenly grown to a much more complex issue encompassing Congress' right to regulate slavery. As Professor David M. Potter put it, the Court "would decide to rush in where Congress had feared to tread."[15]

On February 22, the Court met to discuss *Dred Scott*, but the meeting was short and no conclusions were reached. The Court met again a few days later to consider the case and again failed to reach any conclusions. The justices consulted yet again on April 5, 7, 9, and 12 and still could not reach a decision. Finally, they decided unanimously to reargue the case in the hopes of "clarifying the law and making a final judgment possible."[16] On May 12, the Court ordered the case to be reargued during the next session, in the fall.

By now, many people had begun to question what they perceived to be the Court's political motivation. Some politicians felt the southern Democrats on the Court had deliberately postponed judgment until after the 1856 presidential election so as not to tip the balance in favor of the Republicans. Even Abraham Lincoln expressed the view that southern proslavery Democrats were attempting to sway the Court in the hopes of seeing the Missouri Compromise overturned. This, he felt, would pave the way for the legalization of slavery throughout the country.[17]

James E. Harvey, a reporter for the *New York Tribune*, suggested that the Court had decided to postpone its decision in order to prevent Justice John McLean, a strong supporter of the Missouri Compromise, from delivering a passionate dissent that might launch him into the political arena as the Republican nominee for president of the United States. This argument loses some of its strength, however, from the realization that McLean voted along with the other justices for reargument.

Yet, while some of the justices may have been politically influenced, most simply needed more information before they could reach an informed decision. But it would be seven more months before the case would come once again before the Court—seven long, event-filled months that would help to mold the Court's decision and pave the way for national disaster.

5

To the Court Again

During the seven months before *Dred Scott* v. *Sanford* came up for reargument, the political split between the North and the South grew wider. On May 21, 1856, a large group of proslavery "border ruffians" rode into Lawrence, Kansas, the center of the free-state Kansas Territory, and nearly destroyed the city. The following day, South Carolina's proslavery representative, Preston S. Brooks, physically assaulted Massachusetts' Charles Sumner in response to Sumner's vocal attacks on slavery. Two days later, John Brown launched a raid at Pottawatomie Creek, Kansas, killing five proslavery supporters. It was the first of a long series of violent acts by Brown, who believed that southern slaves could be freed only by force.

As the gap between North and South continued to

grow, the Republicans and Democrats began their campaign for the presidency. The Republicans nominated John C. Fremont and William L. Dayton as their presidential and vice-presidential candidates. Their strong antislavery platform declared that "the Constitution confers upon Congress sovereign power over the Territories of the United States" and that Congress had "both the right and the duty" to prohibit slavery in the territories.[1]

The Democrats, in turn, nominated James Buchanan and John C. Breckinridge under a platform that stressed "popular sovereignty," which called for the question of slavery in the territories to be decided by the residents of those territories. The presidential election of November 4, 1856, resulted in a slim victory for the Democrats and a continuing debate over slavery in Congress.

It was in this politically charged climate that, on December 2, 1856, Henry S. Geyer filed his brief for defendant John Sanford. In response to an order from the Court, Geyer spent a great deal of time talking about the question of citizenship. To be a citizen eligible to sue in the federal courts, according to Geyer, a person had first to be a citizen of the state in which he lived. Missouri did not grant citizenship to blacks—not even free blacks; therefore, Dred Scott was not a citizen.

Geyer also addressed at length the difference between

As conflict between pro and antislavery forces wore on, scenes like this one where police, slaves, and proslavery forces clashed at the Tremont Temple in Boston, MA, were becoming increasingly common.

permanent versus temporary residence. Scott's residence in Illinois was only temporary, he stressed, adding that a slave traveling with his owner in or through a free state is not automatically granted freedom.

On December 15, Montgomery Blair filed an "Additional Brief" to support the one he had filed earlier on behalf of plaintiff Dred Scott. In it, Blair countered Geyer's argument about permanent versus temporary residence. He wrote at length about the constitutionality of the Missouri Compromise. He argued that Congress had had absolute power over U.S. territories since the 1780s. This power, he said, included the right to limit slavery. Since Congress had such power, he concluded, the constitutionality of the Missouri Compromise was not in question.

With both briefs having been submitted, the oral arguments for *Dred Scott* v. *Sanford* were scheduled. All nine justices were present that day, December 15, 1856, and Blair, who by now had been joined by Boston attorney George Ticknor Curtis to help argue the question of the power of Congress over slavery in the territories, opened the arguments for Scott, taking the entire three hours allotted to the case the first day. Blair devoted considerable time to the fact that Dred Scott was a citizen and a proper plaintiff, thus hoping to satisfy the Court on its questions concerning authority.

Next, Blair argued the primary merits, or facts of the case, pointing out first that the states had the absolute right to prohibit slavery and, second, that Congress had the absolute right to make decisions affecting slavery within the territories. Even well-known Southerners such as John C. Calhoun, he said, had accepted the power of Congress to prohibit slavery in the territories. Thus, he said, when Dred Scott came to live in Illinois, he had to be free, since slavery in Illinois had been banned.

On the following day, Geyer argued the case for Sanford. He, like Blair the day before, used all three hours allotted to him, stressing the main point he had made in his brief—that Scott, as a Negro, could not be a citizen of the United States and therefore could not sue in federal court.

Geyer then turned his attention to the facts of the case, arguing that Scott's temporary residence in Illinois did not qualify him for freedom. The Illinois state constitution, he said, simply prevented the state from establishing slavery, but it had no effect on a slave brought into the state, especially if that slave was only passing through the state or living there only temporarily. He insisted this was the case with Dred Scott. He then argued that the Missouri Compromise was a violation of the authority of the people of the United States, since it denied them power over local governments, power which he said the Constitution of the United States had guaranteed them. He concluded the second day's remarks by insisting that Scott could not claim freedom simply because he lived in Illinois. The Missouri Compromise was therefore unconstitutional and thus null and void.

The following day, Reverdy Johnson, also appearing on Sanford's behalf, argued that the Constitution of the United States allowed for the right of citizens to own property, but that it did not consider Negroes to be citizens. Congress, he pointed out, could do nothing that was harmful to any one state. Yet, by prohibiting slavery in the territories, Congress was enacting laws harmful to the interests of the slave states. That was reason enough, he concluded, to find the Missouri Compromise to be unconstitutional.

On the fourth day of oral arguments, all four attorneys addressed the Court. While each supported his previous arguments, Curtis, Scott's new attorney, presented a lengthy discussion of the constitutionality of the Missouri Compromise in Scott's favor. He pointed out that, under Article IV, Section 3 of the Constitution, Congress had the power to "dispose of and make all needful Rules and Regulations respecting the Territory or other Property belonging to the United States." This, Curtis concluded, was proof that the writers of the Constitution had intended from the start that Congress should have absolute power over a territory for as long as it remained a territory. Not until a territory became a state could that state alone have the right to decide upon its institutions, including slavery. Therefore, he concluded, the Missouri Compromise was constitutional, and Dred Scott was entitled to his freedom because he had lived in free Illinois. Curtis' arguments for Scott were both well presented and sound, and Blair must have been grateful at having received such solid last-minute help from so talented a constitutional lawyer.

Yet, at the conclusion of the reargument, all four attorneys realized that the case was out of their hands and under the consideration of the Court, which was now faced with answering four questions placed before it. Two of the questions were procedural and two of them concerned the case's merits, or points of fact.

1. Was there a plea in abatement before the Court? A plea in abatement is a request to throw a case out because it lacks merit. If so, then the Court would refuse to rule on the case. Scott's counsel hoped the Court would decide that there was no plea in abatement.

2. Was Dred Scott a citizen of Missouri and thus able to bring a suit in a federal court? In answering this question, precedent was on Scott's side, since the previous lower court's decision had declared that a free Negro was a citizen under the diverse-citizenship clause. If the Court

The Honorable Henry T. Blow was the representative from Missouri and father of Scott's long-time friend and childhood companion. He would most likely have supported the idea that Dred Scott should be considered a citizen of Missouri and able to fight for his freedom.

decided against Scott on this question, the case would be decided in Sanford's favor. If the Court decided with Scott, the justices would go on to continue the case on its merits.

3. Was Scott a free man because he had lived in Illinois Territory? The answer to this question depended greatly upon whether it found Scott's residence at Fort Armstrong and Fort Snelling to be permanent or merely temporary. If the Court decided in Scott's favor, he would win the case. If it did not, the justices would need to answer the last question.

4. Was Scott a free man because he had lived at Fort Snelling in Minnesota, a free territory as outlined by the Missouri Compromise? An answer to this question would require a ruling on the constitutionality of the Missouri Compromise's restriction on slavery.

Given the strong proslavery makeup of the Court, it seemed likely that its decision would go against Scott. But the Court was concerned with more than making decisions. It was also concerned with the way it reached its decision, something that could have strong political overtones in a nation deeply divided on the question of slavery.

It could avoid a decision entirely, of course, by simply answering the first question positively and the second negatively, thus causing the case to be dismissed for lack of jurisdiction. Jurisdiction is the power, right and authority to interpret and apply the law. That would undoubtedly anger many people opposed to slavery and leave the slavery question up in the air. But the justices were so strongly divided on the question of the plea in abatement that it seemed unlikely that they would take this course.

Another solution would be to uphold the decision of the lower Missouri court, relying on another case, *Strader* v. *Graham*, as a legal precedent. The *Strader* case had involved a group of slaves whose Kentucky owner allowed them to work briefly in Ohio. The Supreme Court had found that the rights of the slaves were based upon the laws of the state from which they had come (Kentucky), rather than upon the laws of Ohio. Once the slaves had returned to Kentucky, they again became the property of their owner. By using the *Strader* principle as the basis for returning negative answers to both questions three and four, the Court would uphold the decision of the lower court, and Scott would lose his bid for freedom.

How would the Court rule? An anxious nation was eager to learn, but only time would tell.

6

The Decision

Christmas, 1856, was a time of mixed feelings for Dred and Harriet Scott. Throughout the course of the Supreme Court hearing, they had worked under the supervision of the Court, which allowed them to be hired out to perform various odd jobs in and around their home in Missouri. The money they made was placed in a bank account to be released following the Court's decision. If the decision went in favor of John Sanford, he would receive the money. If, on the other hand, it went in favor of the Scotts, they would receive the money.

The Scotts had never dreamed that the Court's proceedings would take so long or become so involved. Scott himself later told an interviewer with a local newspaper that he didn't understand what all "the fuss" was about. But fuss there was. In fact, by the time the New Year had dawned, the "great case," which several newspapers had come to call it, had caused heated debate from the local barber shop to the floor of Congress. Everywhere people were talking about *Dred Scott* v. *Sanford*, not because of their interest in the outcome of Scott's bid for freedom so much as from their desire to see how the Court would decide on the question of slavery.

But the Court's decision was unexpectedly delayed when, on January 3, Justice Peter Daniels' wife suffered a horrible death after her clothing caught on fire. The grief-stricken Daniels was unable to attend another session until mid-February, and it was then that the Court held its first conference on *Dred Scott*.

At that conference, two notable things happened. First, Justice Samuel Nelson decided to join four other justices who believed that the plea in abatement was not a consideration of the Court and therefore would not play a role in the Court's decision. This created a majority opinion and was good news for Scott.

Second, the Court's five southern justices favored doing away with the slavery restriction of the Missouri Compromise. Justices McLean and Curtis favored keeping the Compromise intact, while Nelson and Grier favored maintaining the circuit court's decision, thus in effect avoiding entirely a decision on whether or not the Compromise was constitutional. In time, the five southern justices decided to join with Nelson and Grier in upholding the lower court's decision, and Nelson was appointed to write the opinion of the Court. This meant that no decision on the citizenship issue or on the power of Congress to regulate slavery in the territories would be made—more good news for Scott.

But as time passed, the justices became aware that the public had come to expect a decision on the question of the constitutionality of the Missouri Compromise. What had begun as a simple question of ownership had grown into something far more complex. What's more, political pressure from the justices' peers and associates, especially those of the southern justices, was beginning to take its toll. Several members of the Court expressed concerns about the need to save the southern states from the disgrace and humiliation to which Northerners opposed to slavery had been subjecting them. Justice Alexander H. Stephens went so far as to inform his brother that he was urging the Court to a prompt decision, expecting that it would settle the Missouri Compromise issue in the South's favor once and for all.

Even President-elect James Buchanan entered the dispute when he wrote his close friend Justice John Catron on February 3, requesting information on the

William Lloyd Garrison, a famous journalist of the time, began publishing *The Liberator* in 1831. *The Liberator*, a Boston newspaper, spoke out against slavery. The question at hand was whether or not the Court would do the same.

likelihood of the Court's findings. He wanted to know the outcome, he said, so that he could mention the issue in his inaugural address. In fact, Buchanan was hoping that the Court would rule on the constitutionality of the Missouri Compromise so that he could support its findings. Catron's reply of February 10 was disappointing. In his letter, he revealed that the case would be decided as early as Saturday, February 14, and that the Court would probably not make a decision on whether or not Congress had power over slavery in the territories.

But Nelson did not begin work on his opinion until the weekend of February 14-15, when he wrote a short opinion of about five thousand words. In it, Nelson wrote that the Court would not rule on the plea in abatement. About Scott's having lived in Illinois, he wrote that the slave's status as a slave or a free man depended entirely upon where he resided at the time the question was being answered. "The laws of each [state]," he added, "have no extraterritorial operation within the jurisdiction of another [state], except such as may be voluntarily conceded by her laws or courts of justice."[1] If Scott had become free while in Illinois, Nelson reasoned, he did so because Illinois refused to recognize and enforce the slave laws of Missouri. Once he returned to Missouri, however, he returned to that state's laws and to slavery. "Has the law of Illinois any greater force within the jurisdiction of Missouri than the laws of the latter [state] within the former? Certainly not. They stand upon equal footing."[2]

In short, Nelson was saying that the laws of one state were no more or less binding on a person than those of another.

Then Nelson wrote that, once Scott returned from Minnesota to Missouri, the slave state's laws took effect, and Scott was bound by them. Therefore, Scott was still a slave.

No sooner had Nelson concluded his opinion than the Court reversed itself and decided to tackle the much touchier issue of the constitutionality of the Missouri Compromise. The threat of Justices McLean and Curtis to write extensive and damning dissenting opinions disagreeing with all aspects of the case—including the constitutional issue—had forced the Court to reconsider its ruling on the Missouri Compromise. Justice James M. Wayne then moved that Chief Justice Roger B. Taney write the Court's new opinion.

So on March 6, 1857, Taney began reading a shortened summary of his opinion in a crowded courtroom. Following that, Nelson and Catron read their relatively short opinions, and the next day, McLean and Curtis, the two justices in disagreement with the others, read theirs for nearly five hours. But the press had heard little more than it had wanted to hear—the incendiary remarks of the chief justice. The opinion was lavishly praised by southern proslavery Democrats and furiously condemned by northern antislavery Republicans.

When by May 13 Taney's completed opinion had still not been released for publication, Curtis wrote the chief justice and demanded an explanation, declaring his right to examine the Court's official opinion. It was an opinion that Taney was rumored to be revising after hearing the opinions of the two justices in disagreement. Tensions between Curtis and Taney continued to grow as the two sent angry letters back and forth.[3]

Finally, in late May, Taney's official opinion was released, and Curtis was able to compare it to what he remembered of Taney's oral version. He had heard it twice before. Once in conference and then again in Court on March 6. Curtis concluded that "upwards of eighteen pages," or nearly a third of Taney's opinion, had been revised or added. "No one can read them," Curtis said, "without perceiving that they are in reply to my opinion."[4]

Curtis insisted that Taney was wrong in changing his opinion at so late a date, while Taney replied that he had done no such thing. The heated disagreement eventually drove the two justices so far apart that Curtis submitted his resignation from the Court the following September. Publicly, Curtis named the low salary of associate justices as a reason for resigning. In private, however, he admitted to friends that he could not "again feel confidence in the Court and that willingness to cooperate with them which is essential to the satisfactory discharge of my duties."[5]

So the long, drawn-out case of Dred Scott had finally come to an end. The Supreme Court had decided once and for all that Dred Scott was still a slave and that the Missouri Compromise was unconstitutional, a finding that made it null and void. Congress had never had the authority to use slavery or antislavery status as a "measuring stick" for admitting new states into the Union. The ruling had been long awaited and it was distastefully received by many. Now all that remained to be seen were the effects it would have on an already weakened and divided nation. And those effects, it turned out, would be severe.

7
The Aftermath

The impact of the *Dred Scott* decision spread quickly throughout the land. From the papers to the pulpit, from the people to the politicians, everyone had something to say, something to feel about the Court's finding. Those opposed to slavery and the Free-Soilers who, only one day before the verdict, had been working for the release of all slaves suddenly directed their anger toward the Court. They were determined to see *Dred Scott* reversed in order to stop the spread of slavery throughout the country. The best way to do that was through the U.S. Legislature. [1]

By gaining control of the executive and legislative branches of government, the Republicans believed they could place pressure on the Court to reconsider its decision.[2] Better still, with Chief Justice Taney now eighty years old and several other justices not far behind him, it was clear that several members of the Court would soon be leaving, and those who were opposed to slavery wanted a Republican in the White House to nominate antislavery replacements.[3]

Meanwhile, only days after the Court's decision, the *Argus* of Springfield, Massachusetts, printed an article stating that Dred Scott was not actually the property of Alexander Sanford but, rather, of Dr. Calvin Clifford Chaffee, the Republican congressman who had recently married Irene Emerson. In the article, the paper suggested that the antislavery doctor had some serious explaining to do about his relationship to Scott and the most famous Supreme Court case in the land.

In a reply written to the *Springfield Daily Republican* on March 16, 1857, Chaffee wrote that "the defendant [Sanford] was and is the only person who had or has any power in the matter, and neither myself nor any member of my family were consulted in relation to, or even knew of, the existence of the suit till after it was noticed for trial, when we learned of it in an accidental way."[4] When Mrs. Chaffee (formerly Emerson) moved with Mr.Chaffee from St. Louis, she had simply left Scott and his family in the care of her father. It wasn't until February 1857 that she informed her husband that the Dred Scott who was the plaintiff in the Supreme Court

William Lloyd Garrison was one of the many journalists of the time who
had something to say about the Court's findings. His strong antislavery
messages were evident in his many publications.

suit was actually the slave of her deceased husband. "Possessed of no power to control, refused all right to influence the course of the defendant in the cause," Chaffee wrote, he could do nothing to affect the case and was in fact advised by his own attorney to remain quiet until the case had been decided by the Supreme Court.[5]

Now that the Court had given its decision, Chaffee took immediate steps to pave the way for Scott's freedom. On May 26, 1857, he executed a quit claim deed in which he, his wife, and his stepdaughter gave up all rights and interests they may have had in Dred Scott and his family, transferring all rights to Taylor Blow, Scott's long-time friend. Once that was done, Dred and Harriet Scott appeared with Blow in the Missouri Circuit Court, before Judge Alexander Hamilton, and acknowledged the papers granting their freedom. After eleven years of intense legal battles, Dred Scott, his wife, and their daughters were finally free.

Strangely enough, John Sanford never witnessed Scott's freedom. By the time the Supreme Court had rendered its decision, Sanford had been institutionalized for insanity. He died on May 5, 1857. Scott himself, after several weeks of illness and less than two years of freedom, died in St. Louis on Friday, September 17, 1858, and was buried in an unmarked grave in Wesleyan

Cemetery. Nine years later, Taylor Blow had him reburied in the family's plot at Calvary Cemetery in northern St. Louis.

Upon Scott's death in 1858, newspapers around the country carried stories of the most famous slave in the nation. Some, mostly the Republican antislavery papers, rehashed the story of the long and grueling trial that was still tearing the nation apart.

One year later, in October 1859, antislavery activist John Brown, who had murdered five proslavery men during the fighting at Pottawatomie Creek, Kansas, gathered three of his sons and fifteen other followers, both white and black, and staged a daring raid on the federal arsenal at Harpers Ferry, Virginia. Brown succeeded in capturing the arsenal, but his uprising was doomed to failure. Pitting a ragtag band of poorly armed men against a detachment of U.S. Marines under the leadership of Colonel Robert E. Lee and Lieutenant J.E.B. ("Jeb") Stuart proved a disaster.[6]

After a bloody standoff during which the arsenal was subjected to a withering barrage of fire, Brown and eight men who had survived the assault were captured, tried, and convicted. Brown himself was hanged shortly thereafter. Before he died, he wrote a warning to a nation in turmoil:

"I, John Brown, am now quite certain that the crimes of this guilty land will never be purged away but with blood. I had, as I now think, vainly flattered myself that without much bloodshed it might be done."[7]

Meanwhile, during autumn of the previous year, two political candidates from Illinois, a Democrat and a Republican, had agreed to argue the slavery issue in a series of political debates. The Democrat was Stephen A. Douglas, the sponsor of the Kansas-Nebraska Act and a senator running for reelection in Illinois. Douglas was an able leader who hoped someday to become president of the United States.

The Republican challenger for the Senate was antislavery advocate Abraham Lincoln, a lawyer from Springfield, Illinois. Unlike Douglas, Lincoln was unknown outside Illinois. But his friends and neighbors admired his honesty, humor, and ability to win law cases.[8]

Lincoln had spent a great deal of time thinking about the political issues of the day, especially the issue of slavery. In accepting the Republican nomination for the Senate, he had said:

" 'A house divided against itself cannot stand.' I believe this government cannot endure, permanently half slave and half free. I do not expect the Union to be dissolved; I do not expect the house to fall; but I do expect it will cease to be divided. It will become all one thing, or all the other. Either the opponents of slavery will arrest the further spread of it, and place it where the public mind shall rest in the belief that it is in course of ultimate extinction; or its advocates will push it forward, till it shall become alike lawful in all the States, old as well as new, North as well as South."[9]

Those Southerners who heard Lincoln speak were sure that he intended to halt the spread of slavery in the South. They began to fear for their economic livelihood and way of life.[10]

In their debate at Freeport, Illinois, the two men launched arguments that were as different as their political backgrounds. "Should slavery be permitted in the territories?" someone asked. Let the settlers in the territories decide for themselves, said Douglas, arguing for the side of states' rights. Lincoln, on the other hand, supported the rights of the federal government. He suggested slavery could be lawful in the South, but *only* in the South. He wanted slavery kept out of the territories and the newly forming states.[11]

Although neither candidate was a clear winner in the debate, Douglas went on to win the race for the Senate.

Lincoln, on the other hand, won many new friends and loyal supporters for his outspoken views against slavery.

Two years later, as the presidential election year of 1860 drew near, Lincoln was nominated as the Republican party's presidential candidate. In every state, people came to listen to what this outspoken and thoughtful man had to say about the events and issues of the day.

Running against Lincoln for the Democrats was none other than Stephen A. Douglas. But Douglas was having difficulty attracting both northern and southern voters. Voters in the North were leery of him because of his slavery stance in the Lincoln-Douglas debates. After all, Douglas had never come out against slavery, and that bothered many Northerners.[12]

In the South, voters distrusted Douglas because he hadn't clearly stated that slavery should be made legal. Instead, he seemed to straddle the fence by insisting that the settlers of each territory and new state should decide for themselves whether or not they wanted slavery. Many Southerners were still deeply committed to the institution of slavery and simply could not support such a candidate.

As southern Democrats by the thousands turned away from both Lincoln and Douglas, a third man emerged as a political candidate for the presidency. He was John C. Breckinridge of Kentucky. Breckinridge ran on a platform that supported the right to include slavery in all existing territories as well as in all new states.

By the time of the election, Southerners had split in their loyalties. Some voted for Douglas, and some voted for Breckinridge. Meanwhile, Lincoln had won a great majority of the votes in the North, and with them, the presidency of the United States. For the first time in U.S. history, the nation had elected a president who clearly represented the goals and beliefs of only one section of the country, the antislavery North.

Abraham Lincoln was aware of the problems that his victory had created. He understood that the division between North and South was likely to grow worse before it got better. But he was determined to save the Union at any cost. The United States, he believed, had to remain united! [13]

On December 20, 1860, the streets of Charleston, South Carolina, rang out with excitement. Bells chimed. Cheering and singing filled the air. It was as though a huge circus had come to town.

But it was no circus. It was news that South Carolina had just voted to withdraw from the Union, barely one month after Lincoln's election as president. The *Charleston Mercury* newspaper carried the story:

Passed at 1:15 o'clock P.M., December 20, 1860, an ordinance to dissolve the Union between the state of South Carolina, and other states united with her under the compact entitled the Constitution of the United States of America.

A sectional party [the Republican Party] has elected a man [Abraham Lincoln] to the high office of President of the United States whose opinions and purposes are hostile to slavery. He is to be entrusted with the administration of the common government because he has declared that that government cannot endure permanently half slave, half free. "On the fourth of March next this party will take possession of the government. The guarantees of the Constitution will then no longer exist and the equal rights of the states will be lost. The slaveholding states will then no longer have the power of self-government or self-protection, and the federal government will have become their enemy.[14]

Before long, Georgia, Florida, Alabama, Mississippi, Louisiana, and Texas, the states of the Deep South, joined South Carolina in seceding from, or leaving, the Union. On February 4, 1861, representatives of these states met in Montgomery, Alabama, and drew up a constitution of their own for a new nation. The nation was to be called the Confederate States of America. These states modeled their constitution after that of the United States, with one major difference. It stated flatly that no laws could be passed that denied the right to own Negro slaves. Jefferson Davis, who had once fought alongside

Lincoln in the Black Hawk War, was elected president of the Confederacy.

As the date for Abraham Lincoln's inauguration grew closer, people wondered how Lincoln would react to the southern states leaving the Union. Finally, on March 4, 1861, an anxious crowd gathered in Washington, D.C., to hear Lincoln's inaugural address. The new president took his oath of office and began his speech. After the first few words, the audience knew exactly where Lincoln stood:

> "Under the Constitution of the United States, Lincoln said, a permanent Union of the states had been created. None of these states could lawfully leave the Union. It was up to the president to see that the laws of the nation were carried out in all states."

Toward the end of his speech, Lincoln's words turned hopeful as he appealed to the South to return to the Union:

> "In *your* hands, my dissatisfied fellow countrymen, and not in mine, is the momentous issue of civil war. The government will not assail *you*. You can have no conflict without yourselves the aggressors. You have no oath registered in heaven to destroy the government, while *I* shall have the most solemn one to 'preserve, protect, and defend' it. . . .
> "I am loath to close. We are not enemies but friends. We must not be enemies. Though passion may have strained, it must not break our bonds of affection. . . ."[15]

The words had little effect on the South. In the early morning hours of April 12, 1861, a Confederate force led by General Pierre G. T. Beauregard opened fire on Fort Sumter, a United States military post in Charleston, South Carolina. The Civil War had begun.

8
Yesterday, Today, and Tomorrow

Throughout the most bitter Civil War years, President Lincoln continuously clashed with Chief Justice Taney. By now sickly and resentful over popular reaction to his monumental decision, Taney was still certain that he had been correct all along. He was also convinced that Lincoln had gone far beyond the powers of the presidency of the United States and that he needed to be curtailed. [1]

During the next three years, Taney opposed nearly every action taken by Lincoln in the name of the federal government. When Lincoln suspended the writ of habeas corpus, which provides a prisoner with the right to a prompt appearance in court, in an effort to stop the activities of antiwar demonstrators and Confederate sympathizers, Taney objected. He strongly believed that no one could be arrested and imprisoned without a speedy trial, not even during time of war.[2]

When Confederate supporter John Merryman was arrested and brought to Fort McHenry in Baltimore, Taney issued a writ of habeas corpus and ordered General George Cadwalader, the military commander at Fort McHenry, to bring Merryman to the federal court for trial. Cadwalader refused Taney's order because he recognized Lincoln's authority to suspend the right to habeas corpus.

Taney then sent a U.S. marshal to arrest the general for contempt of court. But when the marshal arrived, he was sternly turned away by a military guard. In response, an angry Taney wrote an opinion, *Ex parte Merryman*, in which he declared that only Congress, and not the president, had the power to suspend the right to habeas corpus.[3] Taney sent a copy of his opinion to Lincoln, and Lincoln shared it with his attorney general, who advised the president that Taney was wrong. This angered Taney all the more.[4] Not long after, when the Supreme Court decided in a five to four decision that Lincoln had the power to blockade the southern coast, Taney disagreed. When Lincoln signed the Conscription Act authorizing the drafting of men for war service,

This portrait of the Supreme Court members who presided over the *Dred Scott* case only tells a very small part of the story. While these men may have been responsible for the decision that would eventually spark the Civil War, it was Dred Scott who focused our country's attention on the bigger picture. Slavery was now a source of great debate for people in and out of the legal system.

Taney complained that it was unconstitutional. The chief justice even went so far as to rule against Lincoln's Emancipation Proclamation, which freed the slaves in the Confederacy.

Finally, in 1864, the ongoing war between the cantankerous Taney and the president of the United States came to an end when Chief Justice Taney died at the age of eighty-seven. At a memorial service held by members of the Boston bar, a generous tribute to Taney's long and varied career was delivered by none other than Benjamin R. Curtis, the former Justice who had clashed so often and violently with Taney during the *Dred Scott* case.

In 1868, three years after the Civil War ended in a victory for the Union, Congress passed the Fourteenth Amendment to the Constitution. It declared that Negroes, as well as all other people born or naturalized in the United States, were citizens of the United States and entitled to all citizenship benefits equally. In an ironic twist of fate, it took four years of bloody battle, a presidential proclamation declaring the freedom of enslaved blacks, and a constitutional amendment to overturn the damage that Roger B. Taney and the Supreme Court had done in only a few fateful weeks.

But the freeing of America's slaves and the guarantee of their equal rights of citizenship under the law were not the end of *Dred Scott*. The decision was condemned and criticized by legal historians as a "ghastly error" and a "ruinous decision."[5] Nonetheless, it has paved the groundwork and served as a legal precedent for hundreds of cases ever since, from Reconstruction to civil rights.

For in the end it was not the decision of the Supreme Court or the opinion of Roger Taney; it was not the Civil War or a constitutional amendment; it was not even the Emancipation Proclamation that marked the very first step toward the freeing of America's enslaved blacks. It was the determination of a highly respected man with a strong streak of common sense and a willingness to fight for what he felt was right. It was a man named Dred Scott.

Notes by Chapter

Chapter 1

1. *McCarthy's Weekly Reader*, February 2, 1856.

2. Ibid.

3. Herbert G. Gutman, *Who Built America?* (New York: Pantheon Books, 1989), p. 379.

4. John A. Bryan, "The Blow Family and Their Slave Dred Scott," *Missouri Historical Society Bulletin IV* (July 1948), pp. 223-225; Estate of Peter Blow, Probate Court Records, no. 976, St. Louis.

5. *St. Louis Daily Evening News*, May 26, 1857.

6. John H. Hauberg, "U.S. Army Surgeons at Fort Armstrong," *Journal of the Illinois State Historical Society 24* (January 1932), p. 617.

7. Ibid, p. 619.

8. Emerson file, National Archives, Washington, D.C.

9. Deposition of Miles H. Clark, May 13, 1847, in *Dred Scott* v. *Sanford*, Circuit Court of St. Louis County, Circuit Court, St. Louis, MO.

10. Don E. Fehrenbacher, *The Dred Scott Case: Its Significance in American Law and Politics* (New York: Oxford University Press, 1978), p. 244.

11. Ibid, p. 245.

12. Alfred Brunson, *A Western Pioneer* (Cincinnati: 1873-1879), Vol. II, p. 125.

13. The Dred Scott Collection, The Missouri Historical Society (St. Louis, MO).

Chapter 2

1. Gutman, *Who Built America?* p. 365.

2. Ibid, pp. 365-366.

3. Ibid, p. 385.

Chapter 3

1. Frederick Trevor Hill, *Decisive Battles of the Law* (New York: Fred B. Rothman & Co., 1907), pp. 117-118.

2. *St. Louis Evening News*, April 3, 1857; *St. Louis Globe Democrat*, Jan. 10, 1886.

3. J. Hugo Grimm to Charles Van Ravenswaay, October 29, 1946, citing 1867 records of Calvary Cemetery, Dred Scott Collection, Missouri Historical Society.

4. Walter Ehrlich, "Dred Scott Case," pp. 83-85.

5. *Emmerson v. Harriet (of color)*; *Emmerson v. Dred Scott (of color)*, 11 Missouri 413 (1848); Ehrlich, "Dred Scott Case," pp. 85-87.

6. *Dred Scott v. Emerson*, 15 Missouri 576, pp. 582-587.

7. Ibid.

8. Bond of Taylor Blow, November 2, 1853, and Writ of Summons, November 2, 1853, in *Dred Scott v. Sanford*, no. 692, U.S. Circuit Court at St. Louis.

Chapter 4

1. *St. Louis Morning Herald,* "Interesting Law Case—A Question of Slavery," May 18, 1854.

2. Thomas Lawson, *State Trials,* XIII, pp. 243-245.

3. Ray Allen Billington, *Westward Expansion: A History of the American Frontier* (New York: Macmillan Co., 1974), pp. 274-275.

4. Kenneth C. Davis, *Don't Know Much About History* (New York: Avon Books, 1990), pp. 154-156.

5. *Scott* v. *London,* 3 Cranch 324 (1806); *Lee* v. *Lee,* 8 Peters 44 (1834); *Prigg* v. *State of Pennsylvania,* 16 Peters 539 (1842); *Williams* v. *Ash,* 1 Howard 1 (1843); *Rhodes* v. *Bell,* 2 Howard 397 (1844).

6. *St. Louis Daily Missouri Democrat,* February 25, 1856.

7. *Washington Star,* February 13, 1856, as reported in the *New York Daily Tribune,* February 15, 1856.

8. Ibid.

9. George Brown Tindall, *America: A Narrative History* (New York: W.W. Norton & Co., 1984), p. 600.

10. Fehrenbacher, *The Dred Scott Case,* pp. 300-304.

11. Ibid.

12. *Daily Missouri Democrat,* February 25, 1856.

13. *New York Daily Tribune,* February 18, 1856.

14. *Daily Missouri Republican,* February 21, 1856.

15. David M. Potter, *The Impending Crisis, 1848-1861* (New York, 1976), p. 276.

16. Walter Ehrlich, *They Have No Rights: Dred Scott's*

Struggle for Freedom (Westport, Conn.: Greenwood Press, 1979), p. 102.

17. Ibid, p. 104.

Chapter 5

1. Ehrlich, *They Have No Rights*, p.109.

Chapter 6

1. Fehrenbacher, *The Dred Scott Case*, p. 308.

2. Ibid.

3. Ibid, pp. 316-319.

4. Ibid, p. 319.

5. Frank B. Latham, *The Dred Scott Decision*: March 6, 1857 (New York: Franklin Watts, 1968), p. 32.

Chapter 7

1. Gutman, *Who Built America?*, p. 404.

2. Ibid.

3. Ibid, pp. 404-405.

4. Fehrenbacher, *The Dred Scott Case*, pp. 420-421.

5. *New York Tribune*, March 17, 1857.

6. Gutman, *Who Built America?*, pp. 407-409.

7. Latham, *The Dred Scott Decision*, p. 39.

8. David Wallechinsky and Irving Wallace, *The People's Almanac* (Garden City, NY: Doubleday & Co., 1975), p. 285.

9. Davis, *Don't Know Much About History*, p. 160.

10. Gutman, *Who Built America?*, p. 407.

11. Ibid, p. 422.

12. Davis, *Don't Know Much About History*, pp. 158-161.

13. Tindall, *America: A Narrative History*, p. 619.

14. Ibid, p. 613.

15. Davis, *Don't Know Much About History*, p. 165.

Chapter 8

1. Fehrenbacher, *The Dred Scott Case*, pp. 521-522.

2. Ibid.

3. Geoffrey C. Ward, *The Civil War: An Illustrated History* (New York: Alfred A. Knopf, 1991), p. 61.

4. Fehrenbacher, *The Dred Scott Case*, pp. 574-575.

5. Alexander M. Bickel, *The Supreme Court and the Idea of Progress* (New York: Macmillan Co., 1970), p. 41.

Further Reading

Ehrlich, Walter, *They Have No Rights: Dred Scott's Struggle for Freedom.* Westport, Conn.: Greenwood Press, 1979.

Fehrenbacher, Don E., *The Dred Scott Case: Its Significance in American Law and Politics.* New York: Oxford University Press, 1978.

Latham, Frank B., *The Dred Scott Decision: March 6, 1857.* New York: Franklin Watts, 1968.

Lawson, Don, *Landmark Supreme Court Cases.* Hillside, NJ: Enslow Publishers, 1987.

Weiss, Ann, *The Supreme Court.* Hillside, NJ: Enslow Publishers, 1987.

Index

About the Author

D.J. Herda is a widely published author of over 60 books for young people. In addition to his career as a writer, Mr. Herda is an accomplished photographer, painter, and sculptor whose works currently appear in galleries and shows throughout North America.